How Many Months?

by Katherine Krieg

amicus readers 2

amicus readers

Say Hello to Amicus Readers.

You'll find our helpful dog, Amicus, chasing a ball—to let you know the reading level of a book.

1 Learn to Read

Frequent repetition, high frequency words, and close photo-text matches introduce familiar topics and provide ample support for brand new readers.

2 Read Independently

Some repetition is mixed with varied sentence structures and a select amount of new vocabulary words are introduced with text and photo support.

3 Read to Know More

Interesting facts and engaging art and photos give fluent readers fun books both for reading practice and to learn about new topics.

Amicus Readers are published by Amicus
P.O. Box 1329, Mankato, MN 56002
www.amicuspublishing.us

Photo Credits: iStockphoto, cover, 6, 11; CE Futcher/iStockphoto, 1; Benjamin Albiach Galan/Shutterstock Images, 3; Vikram Raghuvanshi/iStockphoto, 5; Steve Bower/Shutterstock Images, 8; Shutterstock Images, 12–13; Yuriy S./iStockphoto, 14–15; Ria Wonder/Shutterstock Images, 16

Produced for Amicus by The Peterson Publishing Company and Red Line Editorial.

Editor Jenna Gleisner
Designer Becky Daum

Library of Congress
Cataloging-in-Publication Data
Krieg, Katherine, author.
How many months? / by Katherine Krieg.
pages cm. -- (Amicus readers level 2) (Measuring time)
Summary: "Introduces activities young readers experience in a matter of months, such as learning a new sport, while teaching ways to measure a month and how it compares to weeks and years."-- Provided by publisher.
Audience: K to grade 3
ISBN 978-1-60753-725-0 (library binding)
ISBN 978-1-60753-829-5 (ebook)
1. Time--Juvenile literature. 2. Time measurements--Juvenile literature. I. Title.
QB209.5.K754 2014
529.7--dc23

2014049951

Printed in Malaysia
10 9 8 7 6 5 4 3 2 1

We use months to measure time. A month is about 4 weeks long. The shortest month is 28 days. The longest is 31 days.

School starts in the month of September. Cam gets a haircut. His hair grew about one-half inch in

1 month.

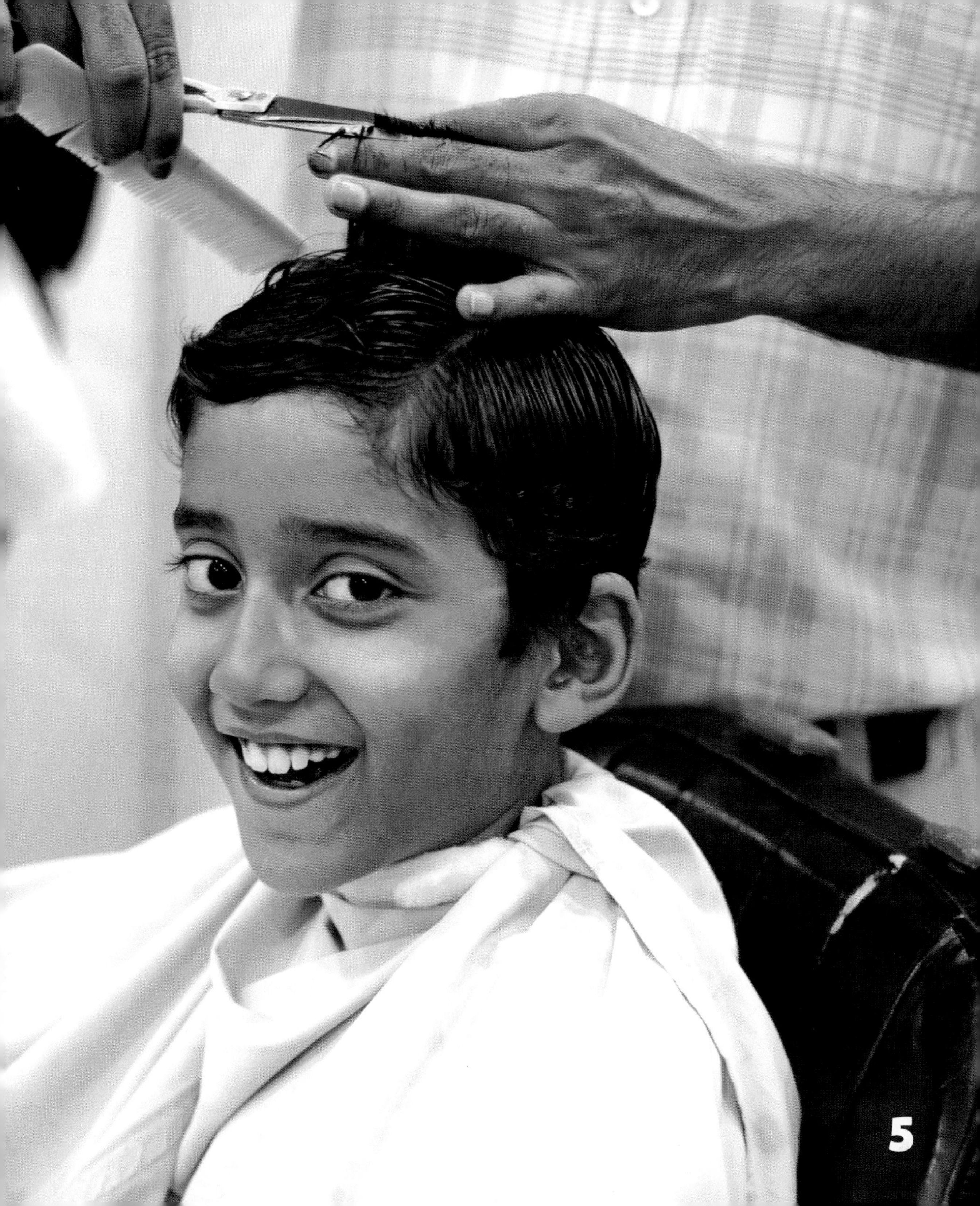

Rosa learns how to read the calendar. There are 12 months in a year. Each month is 1 page on the calendar. Rosa counts

2 months

until her birthday in November.

Beau plays baseball after school. His baseball season lasts **3 months.**

Ali goes to piano lessons after school. In 6 months, she will have her first recital. That is half of 1 year.

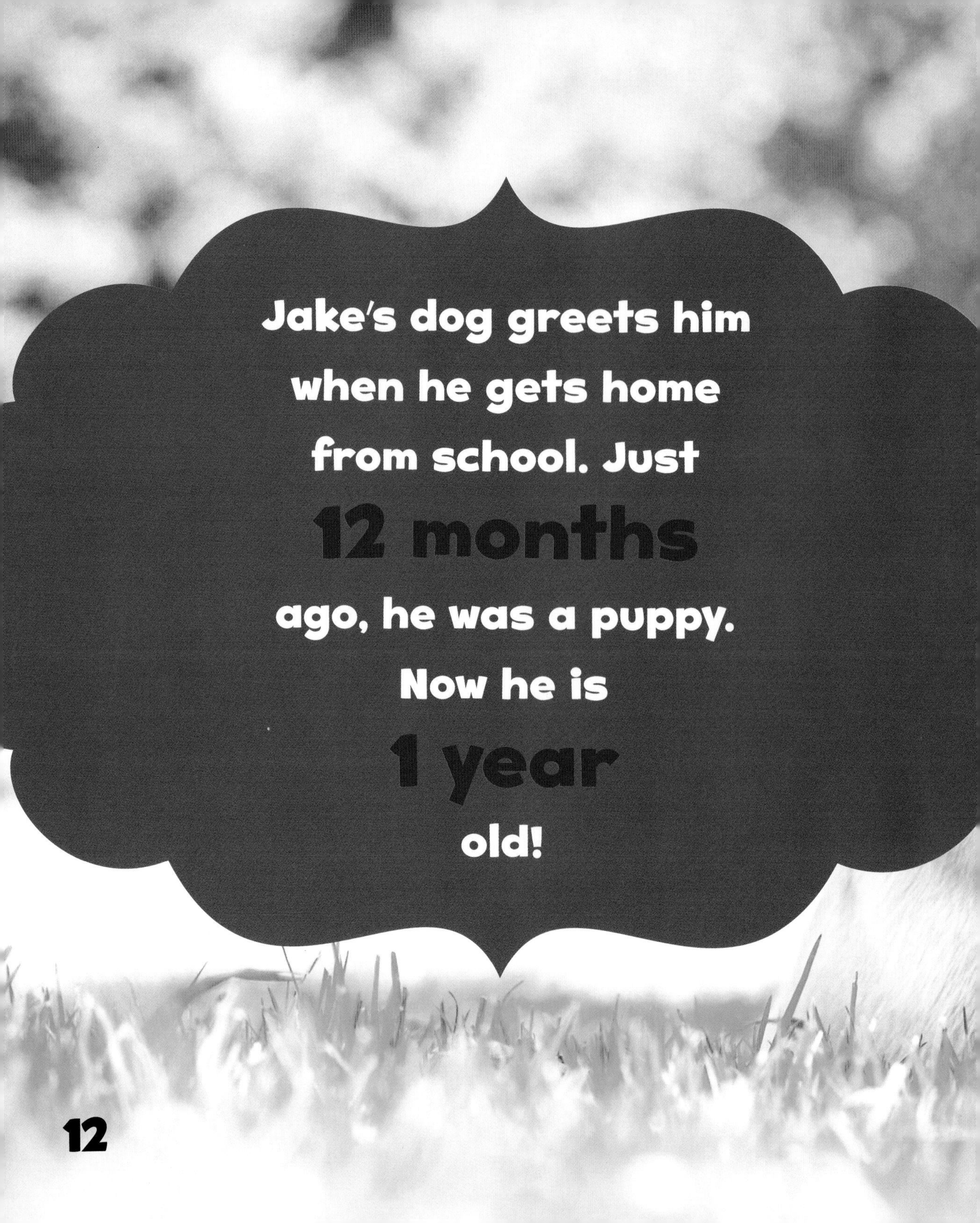

Jake's dog greets him when he gets home from school. Just

12 months

ago, he was a puppy. Now he is

1 year

old!

A lot can happen in just 1 month.

How many months is it until your birthday?

Measuring Months

January

Mo	Tu	We	Th	Fr	Sa	Su
					1	2
3	4	5	6	7	8	9
10	11	12	13	14	15	16
17	18	19	20	21	22	23
24	25	26	27	28	29	30
31						

February

Mo	Tu	We	Th	Fr	Sa	Su
	1	2	3	4	5	6
7	8	9	10	11	12	13
14	15	16	17	18	19	20
21	22	23	24	25	26	27
28						

March

Mo	Tu	We	Th	Fr	Sa	Su
	1	2	3	4	5	6
7	8	9	10	11	12	13
14	15	16	17	18	19	20
21	22	23	24	25	26	27
28	29	30	31			

1 week

April

Mo	Tu	We	Th	Fr	Sa	Su
				1	2	3
4	5	6	7	8	9	10
11	12	13	14	15	16	17
18	19	20	21	22	23	24
25	26	27	28	29	30	

May

Mo	Tu	We	Th	Fr	Sa	Su
						1
2	3	4	5	6	7	8
9	10	11	12	13	14	15
16	17	18	19	20	21	22
23	24	25	26	27	28	29
30	31					

June

Mo	Tu	We	Th	Fr	Sa	Su
		1	2	3	4	5
6	7	8	9	10	11	12
13	14	15	16	17	18	19
20	21	22	23	24	25	26
27	28	29	30			

July

Mo	Tu	We	Th	Fr	Sa	Su
				1	2	3
4	5	6	7	8	9	10
11	12	13	14	15	16	17
18	19	20	21	22	23	24
25	26	27	28	29	30	31

August

Mo	Tu	We	Th	Fr	Sa	Su
1	2	3	4	5	6	7
8	9	10	11	12	13	14
15	16	17	18	19	20	21
22	23	24	25	26	27	28
29	30	31				

September

Mo	Tu	We	Th	Fr	Sa	Su
			1	2	3	4
5	6	7	8	9	10	11
12	13	14	15	16	17	18
19	20	21	22	23	24	25
26	27	28	29	30		

October

Mo	Tu	We	Th	Fr	Sa	Su
					1	2
3	4	5	6	7	8	9
10	11	12	13	14	15	16
17	18	19	20	21	22	23
24	25	26	27	28	29	30
31						

November

Mo	Tu	We	Th	Fr	Sa	Su
	1	2	3	4	5	6
7	8	9	10	11	12	13
14	15	16	17	18	19	20
21	22	23	24	25	26	27
28	29	30				

December

Mo	Tu	We	Th	Fr	Sa	Su
			1	2	3	4
5	6	7	8	9	10	11
12	13	14	15	16	17	18
19	20	21	22	23	24	25
26	27	28	29	30	31	

1 year

1 month